SCAN & SING 2

How To Use This Book

Thank you for purchasing Scan & Sing 2! Scan & Sing 2 includes QR codes for 500 popular karaoke songs absent from first book. We also collected new links to karaoke songs from popular artists since we published. This book is arguably as essential as the first volume. If you like to Scan & Sing, leave us an Amazon review or email us at dreamingtreepublishing@gmail.com!

See our other products at https://scanand.store

1. Choose a Song

Use the Table of Contents to find a song you'd like to perform. Songs are organized alphabetically by artist.

2. Scan a Song With Your Phone

Use your smartphone's camera or a QR code/barcode reader application to scan and launch a song's associated karaoke video.

3. Screenshare or Cast to Your TV

Using Chromecast or other screensharing software, cast your chosen video to your screen, and get ready to perform!

Scan & Sing Karaoke Book

3 Doors Down

Kryptonite

3 Doors Down

When I'm Gone

Abba

Take a Chance on Me

AC/DC

Dirty Deeds Done Dirt Cheap

Adele

Easy On Me

Adele

Rolling in the Deep

Adele
Rumor Has It

Aerosmith
Jaded

Aerosmith
Walk This Way

Aerosmith
Cryin'

Aerosmith
Dream On

Air Supply
Chances

Alessia Cara

How Far I'll Go

Alex Clare

Too Close

America

Sister Golden Hair

Anne Murray

I Just Fall In Love Again

Aqua

Barbie Girl

Aretha Franklin

I Say a Little Prayer

Ariana Grande

7 Rings

Ariana Grande

One Last Time

Ariana Grande

Breathin'

Ariana Grande

Tattooed Heart

Ariana Grande, John Legend

Beauty & The Beast

Audioslave

Like a Stone

Audrey Hepburn

Moon River

Auli'i Cravalho

How Far I'll Go

Ava Max

Kings & Queens

Ava Max

Sweet But Psycho

Ava Max

So Am I

Avirl Lavigne

Complicated

Avirl Lavigne

I'm With You

Avirl Lavigne

Sk8er Boi

Avirl Lavigne

My Happy Ending

Avirl Lavigne

Girlfriend

Avirl Lavigne

When You're Gone

B.J. Thomas

Raindrops Keep Falling on My Head

Bad Bunny

Yonaguni

Bad Bunny

Moscow Mule

Bad Bunny

Callaíta

Beatles

In My Life

Bee Gees

To Love Somebody

Beyonce

Single Ladies

Beyonce

Pretty Hurts

Beyonce

Cuff It

Beyonce

I Was Here

Beyonce

Break My Soul

Beyonce & Jay-Z

Drunk In Love

Big Star

Thirteen

Billie Eilish

lovely (with Khalid)

Billie Eilish

idontwannabeyouanymore

Billie Eilish

i love you

Blondie

Heart of Glass

Blondie

One Way Or Another

Blue Öyster Cult

Don't Fear the Reaper

Blue Swede, Bjorn Skifs

Hooked on a Feeling

Bo Burnham

"1985"

Bob Dylan

Like a Rolling Stone

Bob Dylan

Hey, Mr. Tambourine Man

Bob Dylan

The Times, They Are A-Changin'

Bob Dylan

Knockin' On Heaven's Door

Bob Seger

Turn The Page

Bob Seger

Against The Wind

Bob Seger

Night Moves

Bob Seger

Old TIme Rock & Roll

Bob Seger

Like a Rock

Bon Jovi

Livin' On A Prayer

Brian McKnight

One Last Cry

Brian McKnight

Back At One

Bruno Mars

Talking To The Moon

Bryan Adams

Everything I Do (I Do It For You)

Bryan Adams

Please Forgive Me

BTS

Dynamite

BTS

Permission to Dance

BTS

Butter

BTS

Life Goes On

Buddy Holly

That'll Be The Day

Bush

Glycerine

Carl Douglas

Kung Fu Fighting

Carly Simon

You're So Vain

Carpenters

We've Only Just Begun

Carpenters

I Won't Last A Day Without You

Chainsmoker ft. Kelsea Ballerini

This Feeling

Chainsmokers

Paris

Chainsmokers ft. Coldplay

Somthing Just Like This

Chainsmokers ft. Daya

Don't Let Me Down

Chainsmokers ft. Halsey

Closer

Chainsmokers ft. Lennon Stella

Illenium

Chainsmokers ft. Phoebe Ryan

All We Know

Chainsmokers ft. Rozes

Roses

Charlie Puth

Attention

Charlie Puth

How Long

Charlie Puth

That's Hilarious

Charlie Puth

Light Switch

Charlie Puth

The Way I Am

Cher

You Haven't Seen The Last Of Me

Chris DeBurgh

Lady In Red

Chris Stapleton

Tennessee Whiskey

Chubby Checker

Let's Twist Again

Chuck Berry

You Never Can Tell

Counting Crows

Mr. Jones

Creed

My Sacrifice

Creed

Higher

Creed
One Last Breath

Creed
With Arms Wide Open

Creedence Clearwater Revival
Jambalaya

Cults
Always Forever

Daniel Powter
Bad Day

David Bowie
Ziggy Stardust

Dean Martin

Sway

Del Shannon

Runaway

Demi Lovato

Heart Attack

Demi Lovato

Stone Cold

Demi Lovato

La La Land

Demi Lovato

Skyscraper

Demi Lovato

Don't Forget

Demi Lovato

Warrior

Demi Lovato

Give Your Heart a Break

Demi Lovato

Anyone

Demi Lovato

Wihtout the Love

Demi Lovato

Neon Lights

Depeche Mode

Personal Jesus

Depeche Mode

Enjoy the Silence

Destiny's Child

Emotion

Dion

The Wanderer

Dion & The Belmonts

Teenager in Love

DNCE

Cake by the Ocean

Doja Cat

Streets

Doja Cat

Say So

Doja Cat

Woman

Doja Cat ft. SZA

Kiss Me More

Doja Cat, The Weeknd

You Right

Donna Lewis

I Love You Always Forever

Donna Summer

Hot Stuff

Dua Lipa

IDGAF

Dua Lipa

New Rules

Dua Lipa

Don't Start Now

Dua Lipa

Love Again

Dua Lipa

Break My Heart

Dusty Springfield

You Don't Have To Say You Love Me

Earth, Wind and Fire

September

Eiffel 65

Blue

Ellie Goulding

Love Me Like You Do

Ellie Goulding

Burn

Ellie Goulding

Lights

Ellie Goulding

Still Falling For You

Ellie Goulding

On My Mind

Ellie Goulding

Army

Elliot Smith

Between the Bars

Elliot Smith

Angeles

Elliot Smith

Somebody That I Used To Know

Elliot Smith

A Fond Farewell

Elliot Smith

Waltz #2

Elliot Smith

Son of Sam

Elliot Smith

Everything Reminds Me of Her

Elvis Presley

It's Now Or Never

Elvis Presley

Can't Help Falling In Love

Elvis Presley
If I Can Dream

Elvis Presley
Jailhouse Rock

Elvis Presley
Hound Dog

Elvis Presley
Suspicious Minds

Elvis Presley
Don't Be Cruel

Elvis Presley
That's All Right

Elvis Presley

It's Now Or Never

Elvis Presley

Always On My Mind

Eminem

Mockingbird

Encanto

We Don't Talk About Bruno

Enrique Iglesias

Hero

Everly Brothers

Crying In The Rain

Fifth Harmony

Worth It

Fifth Harmony

I'm in Love with a Monster

Fifth Harmony

Miss Movin' On

Fifth Harmony

Bo$$

Fifth Harmony ft. Ty Dolla Sign

Work From Home

Flo Rida

Whistle

Flo Rida

My House

Flo Rida

Good Feeling

Flo Rida, David Guetta

Club Can't Handle Me

Flo Rida, Ke$ha

Right Round

Flo Rida, T-Pain

Low

Foreigner

I Want To Know What Love Is

Frank Sinatra

Come Fly With Me

Frankie Valli and the Four Seasons

I Can't Take My Eyes Off You

Frankie Valli and the Four Seasons

Sherry

Frankie Valli and the Four Seasons

Bye Bye Baby (Baby Goodbye)

Frankie Valli and the Four Seasons

Walk Like a Man

Garbage

Only Happy When It Rains

GAYLE

abcdefu

Gazebo

I Like Chopin

George Ezra

Budapest

Gordon Lightfoot

Wreck of the Edmund Fitzgerald

Gorillaz

Feel Good, Inc

Gorillaz

Clint Eastwood

Gotye and Kimbra

Somebody That I Used To Know

Guns N' Roses

Patience

Guns N' Roses

Don't Cry

Guns N' Roses

November Rain

Guns N' Roses

Welcome to the Jungle

Guns N' Roses

Sweet Child of Mine

Hall & Oates

Maneater

Hall/Oates

You Make My Dreams Come True

Halsey

Without Me

Halsey

Bad at Love

Halsey

You Should Be Sad

Halsey

Colors

Halsey

Gasoline

Halsey

So Good

Halsey

Castle

Halsey

Eyes Closed

Hank WIlliams, Jr.

Your Cheatin' Heart

Harry Chapin

Cat's In The Cradle

Harry Chapin

I Wanna Learn a Love Song

Harry Chapin

Better Place To Be

Harry Chapin

Taxi

Harry Styles

Falling

Harry Styles

As It Was

Harry Stylez

Sweet Creatures

Harry Stylez

Kiwi

Harry Stylez

Watermelon Sugar

Harry Stylez

Adore You

Harry Stylez

Matilda

Harry Stylez

Boyfriends

Imagine Dragons

Believer

Imagine Dragons

Sharks

Imagine Dragons

Thunder

Imagine Dragons

Radioactive

Israel Kamakawiwo'ole

Over The Rainbow / What a Wonderful World

James Blunt

You're Beautiful

James Brown

I Got You (I Feel Good)

James Brown

Papa's Got A Brand New Bag

James Brown

It's a Man's Man's Man's World

James Brown

Get Up Offa That Thing

James Taylor

Fire and Rain

Jax

I Know Victoria's Secret

Jessie J

Who You Are

39

Jessie J
Masterpiece

Jessie J
Domino

Jessie J ft. B.o.B
Price Tag

Jessie J, Ariana Grande, Nicki Minaj
Bang Bang

Jim Croce
I Got a Name

Jim Croce
Time In A Bottle

40

Jim Croce
I'll Have To Say I Love You In A Song

Jimi Hendrix
All Along the Watchtower

Jimi Hendrix
Purple Haze

Jimi Hendrix
Voodoo Child

Jimmy Cliff
I Can See Clearly Now

John Mellencamp
Hurts So Good

Joji

Test Drive

Joji

Glimpse of Us

Joji

Sanctuary

Judy Garland

Somewhere Over the Rainbow

Juice WRLD

Lucid Dreams

JVKE

Upside Down

JVKE

This is What Heartbreak Feels Like

JVKE

Golden Hour

JVKE

This is What Falling in Love Feels Like

Kansas

Dust In The Wind

Kate Bush

Running Up That Hill

Katy Perry

Last Friday Night (T.G.I.F.)

Katy Perry

E.T.

Katy Perry

The One That Got Away

Katy Perry

I Kissed a Girl

Katy Perry

Dark Horse

KC And The Sunshine Band

That's The Way (I Like It)

Ke$ha

TiK ToK

Ke$ha

Praying

Keane

She Has No Time

Keane

Bedshaped

Keane

Bend and Break

Keane

We Might As Well Be Strangers

KISS

I Was Made For Lovin' You

45

KISS

Rock and Roll All Nite

KT Tunstall

Suddenly I See

KT Tunstall

Black Horse and a Cherry Tree

Lady Gaga

Always Remember Us This Way

Lauper

Girls Just Want to Have Fun

Led Zeppelin

Stairway To Heaven

Lemon Tree

Fool's Garden

Lil Nas X

That's What I Want

Lil Nas X

Sun Goes Down

Lil Nas X

Panini

Lil Nas X ft Jack Harlow

Industry Baby

Lionel Richie

Hello

Lionel Richie

Hello

Little Richard

Tutti Frutti

Louis Armstrong

What a Wonderful World

Luther Vandross

Dance With My Father

Lynyrd Skynyrd

Simple Man

Macklemore & Ryan Lewis

Downtown

Macklemore & Ryan Lewis

Can't Hold Us

Macklemore & Ryan Lewis

Downtown

Macklemore & Ryan Lewis

Thrift Shop

Macklemore & Ryan Lewis

Same Love

Manfred Mann

Blinded By The Light

Marvin Gaye, Tammi Terrell

Ain't No Mountain High Enough

Metallica

Nothing Else Matters

Michael Jackson

Billie Jean

Michael Jackson

Bad

Michael Jackson

Beat It

Michael Jackson

Smooth Criminal

Michael Jackson

Man in the Mirror

Michael Jackson

The Way You Make Me Feel

Michael Jackson

Thriller

Mumford and Sons

The Cave

Mumford and Sons

Awake My Soul

Niall Horan

Slow Hands

Niall Horan

This Town

Niall Horan

Too Much to Ask

Niall Horan

Flicker

Niall Horan

No Judgement

Nickelback

How You Remind Me

Nickelback

Rockstar

Nickelback

Photograph

Nicki Minaj

Super Bass

Nicki Minaj

Anaconda

Nicki Minaj

Chun-Li

Nicki Minaj

Starships

Nicki Minaj

Super Freaky Girl

Nirvana

Smells Like Teen Spirit

Nirvana

Come As You Are

Nirvana

In Bloom

Nirvana

Come As You Are

Nirvana

Smells Like Teen Spirit

Nitty Gritty Dirt Band

Mr. Bojangles

Norman Greenbaum

Spirit in the Sky

Olivia Rodrigo

happier

Olivia Rodrigo

All I Want

Olivia Rodrigo

favorite crime

Olivia Rodrigo

traitor

Olivia Rodrigo

good 4 u

Olivia Rodrigo

1 step forward, 3 steps back

Olivia Rodrigo

jealousy, jealousy

Olivia Rodrigo

brutal

One Direction

Kiss You

One Direction

Night Changes

One Direction

Best Song Ever

One Direction

More Than This

One Direction

Steal My Girl

One Direction

Love You Goodbye

One Direction

Infinity

One Republic

I Ain't Worried

P!nk

Raise Your Glass

P!nk

So What

P!nk

Try

P!nk

Sober

P!nk

Who Knew

P!nk

What About Us

Panic! at the Disco

I Write Sins Not Tragedies

Panic! at the Disco

Death of a Bachelor

Panic! at the Disco

The Ballad of Mona Lisa

Panic! at the Disco

Nine in the Afternoon

Panic! at the Disco

Girls/Girls/Boys

Panic! at the Disco

Always

Pat Benatar

Hit Me With Your Best Shot

Pat Benatar

We Belong

Pat Benatar

Love is a Battlefield

Paul Anka

Put Your Head On My Shoulder

Peaches & Herb

Shake Your Groove Thing

Petula Clark

Downtown

Pharrell Williams

Happy

Pharrell Williams

Freedom

Pitbull and Ke$ha

Timber

Poison

Every Rose Has Its Thorn (With Lyrics)

Portugal the Man

Feel It Still

Post Malone

Circles

Post Malone, Swae Lee

Sunflower

Prince

Kiss

R.E.M.

The One I Love

R.E.O. Speedwagon

Can't Fight This Feeling Anymore

Redbone

Come and Get Your Love

Right Said Fred

I'm Too Sexy

Rihanna

Love On The Brain

Rihanna, Mikky Ekko

Stay

Rolling Stones

You Can't Always Get What You Want

Rolling Stones

Paint It Black

Rolling Stones

Beast of Burden

Roxette

Listen to Your Heart

Roy Orbison

Oh, Pretty Woman

Roy Orbison

Crying

Roy Orbison

You Got It

Roy Orbison

Only The Lonely

Rupert Holmes

Escape (The Pina Colada Song)

Sam Smith

I'm Not The Only One

Sam Smith

Stay With Me

Sam Smith

Lay Me Down

Sam Smith

Too Good At Goodbyes

Sam Smith

Writing's On The Wall

Sam Smith

How Do You Sleep

Sam Smith

Like I Can

Sam Smith

Praying

Sara Bareilles

Gravity

Sara Bareilles

She Used to Be Mine

Sara Bareilles

I Choose You

Sara Bareilles

Brave

Savage Garden

I Knew I Loved You

Seal

Kiss From a Rose

Selena

Dreaming of You

Selena Gomez

Slow Down

Selena Gomez

Hands to Myself

Selena Gomez

Kill Em With Kindness

Selena Gomez, Charlie Puth

We Don't Talk Anymore

Selena Gomez, Marshmello

Wolves

Selena Gomez, Rema

Calm Down

Selena Gomez, The Scene

A Year Without Rain

Shakira

Whenever, Wherever

Shakira

Hips Don't Lie

Shakira

Try Everything

Shakira

Underneath Your Clothes

Sia

Cheap Thrills

Sia

Snowman

Sia

Unstoppable

Sia

Elastic Heart

Sia

Fire Meet Gasoline

Sinead O'Connor

Nothing Compares 2 U

Sisqo

Incomplete

Starship

Nothing's Gonna Stop Us Now

Steve Lacy

Bad Habit

Steve Lacy

Dark Red

Stevie Wonder

I Just Called To Say I Love You

Stevie Wonder

Superstition

Stevie Wonder

My Cheri Amour

Stevie Wonder

Lately

Stevie Wonder

Signed, Sealed, Delivered I'm Yours

Sting

Shape of My Heart

Sting

Fields of Gold

Sting

Englishman in New York

Stone Temple Pilots

Plush

Stone Temple Pilots

Sour Girl

Stone Temple Pilots

Interstate Love Song

Stone Temple Pilots

Vaseline

Supertramp

The Logical Song

Sweet Dreams (are made of this)

Eurythmics

System of a Down

Lonely Day

System of a Down

Toxicity

The Animals

Don't Let Me Be
Misunderstood

The Archies

Sugar Sugar

The Beatles

The Long and Winding Road

The Cascades

Rhythm of the Rain

The Clash

Should I Stay Or Should I Go

The Clash

I Fought The Law

The Cranberries

Zombie

The Doors

Riders On The Storm

The Doors

Break On Through

The Five Stairsteps

O-o-h Child

The Go-Go's

Vacation

The Go-Go's

Our Lips Are Sealed

The Go-Go's

We Got the Beat

The Jonas Brothers

Burnin' Up

The Jonas Brothers

SOS

The Jonas Brothers

Lovebug

The Jonas Brothers

Year 3000

The Killers

Smile Like You Mean It

The Killers

Human

The Killers

Jenny Was a Friend of Mine

The Lovin' Spoonful

Do You Believe in Magic

The Mamas and the Papas

Dream a Little Dream of Me

The Mommas and the Papas

California Dreamin'

The Platters

Only You (And You Alone)

The Police

Roxanne

The Ramones

I Wanna Be Sedated

The Ramones

Blitzkrieg Bop

The Righteous Brothers

Unchained Melody

The Rolling Stones

Gimme Shelter

The Ronettes

Be My Baby

The Smiths

There Is A Light That Never Goes Out

The Smiths

This Charming Man

The Smiths

Heaven Knows I'm Miserable Now

The Smiths

How Soon Is Now

The Verve

Bitter Sweet Symphony

The Wanted

Glad You Came

The Wanted

Chasing the Sun

The Wanted

We Own the Night

The Wanted

I Found You

The White Stripes

Seven Nation Army

The White Stripes

Fell In Love With a Girl

The White Stripes

The Hardest Button To Button

The Who

Pinball Wizard

The Who

Baba O'Riley

They Might Be Giants

Experimental Film

Thin Lizzy

The Boys are Back in Town

Timbaland, One Republic

Apologize

Tina Turner

What's Love Got To Do With It

Tina Turner

The Best

Tones & I

Fly Away

Train

Drops of Jupiter

Twenty One Pilots

Chlorine

Twenty One Pilots

Car Radio

Twenty One Pilots

Migraine

Twenty One Pilots

Tear in My Heart

Twenty One Pilots

Heathens

U2

Sunday, Bloody Sunday

Usher, Alicia Keys

My Boo

Vanilla Ice

Ice Ice Baby

Vertical Horizon
Everything You Want

Village People
YMCA

Weezer
Say it Ain't So

Weezer
Undone (The Sweater Song)

Weezer
Buddy Holly

Westlife
If I Let You Go

XXXTENTACION

Changes

Made in United States
Orlando, FL
09 December 2024

55312428R00057